Yellow Umbrella Books are published by Capstone Press
151 Good Counsel Drive, P.O. Box 669, Mankato, Minnesota 56002
www.capstonepress.com

Library of Congress Cataloging-in-Publication Data
Ring, Susan.
　　From here to there / Susan Ring.
　　p. cm.
　　Summary: Photographs and simple text explore the different modes of
transportation used by people around the world.
　　ISBN 0-7368-2908-3 (hardcover)—ISBN 0-7368-2867-2 (softcover)
　　1. Transportation—Juvenile literature. [1. Transportation.] I. Title.
HE152.R56 2004
388—dc22　　　　　　　　　　　　　　　　　　　　2003007743

Editorial Credits
Editorial Director: Mary Lindeen
Editor: Jennifer VanVoorst
Photo Researcher: Deirdre Barton, Wanda Winch
Developer: Raindrop Publishing

Photo Credits
Cover: Earl and Nazima Kowall/Corbis; Title Page: Corel; Page 2: DigitalVision; Page
3: Ric Ergenbright/Corbis; Page 4: EyeWire/PhotoDisc; Page 5: Corel; Page 6: John
Foxx; Page 7: DigitalVision; Page 8: Jacques Langevin/Corbis Sygma; Page 9:
Comstock; Page 10: Corel; Page 11: Annie Reynolds/PhotoLink/PhotoDisc; Page 12:
Royalty-Free/Corbis; Page 13: Royalty-Free/Corbis; Page 14: Royalty-Free/Corbis;
Page 15: Art Stein/Corbis; Page 16: Goodshoot

1 2 3 4 5 6 09 08 07 06 05 04

From Here to There

by Susan Ring

Consultant: Dwight Herold, EdD, Past President,
Iowa Council for the Social Studies

Yellow Umbrella Books

an imprint of Capstone Press
Mankato, Minnesota

How do people get around
and go from here to there?

They might take a hot air
balloon up high into the air.

They might use a boat to sail
or maybe one to row.

They might use a dogsled
to pull them through the snow.

They might fly a jet
and soar up in the sky.

They might fly the space shuttle
and see the Earth go by.

Some people ride in buses
that take them very far.

Some people travel here and there by riding in a car.

A horse that pulls you in a cart can get you to the market.

A bike can also get you there,
and it's easier to park it!

A cable car will take you
down a very busy street.

A taxi takes you downtown
while you're buckled
in your seat.

The people in this city ride boats to get around.

The people in this city ride trains deep underground.

How do people get around
and go from here to there?
There are so many different
ways to get you anywhere!

Words to Know/Index

bike—a vehicle with two wheels, handlebars for steering, and pedals for pedaling; page 11

cable car—a vehicle pulled along by a moving cable, used for carrying people along city streets or up mountains; page 12

dogsled—a vehicle with metal runners pulled over ice and snow by dogs; page 5

hot air balloon—an aircraft with a very large bag filled with hot air or gas; a hot air balloon has a basket for carrying passengers; page 3

jet—an aircraft powered by jet engines; page 6

market—a place where people buy and sell food or goods; page 10

shuttle—a spacecraft that carries astronauts into space and back to earth; page 7

taxi—a car with a driver that passengers pay to take them where they want to go; page 13

Word Count: 179
Early-Intervention Level: 11

CRANBURY PUBLIC LIBRARY
23 North Main Street
Cranbury, NJ 08512
609-655-0555

NO 20 06